Noam Chomsky: A Life of Critical Inquiry and Social Transformation

Noam Chomsky, an intellectual luminary and renowned thinker of our time, was born into an intellectual Jewish family on December 7, 1928, in the vibrant city of Philadelphia. His parents, William and Elsie Chomsky, both hailed from modest backgrounds but possessed an insatiable thirst for knowledge, a trait that would profoundly influence their son's trajectory.

William Chomsky, a distinguished Hebrew scholar and author, instilled in young Noam a deep appreciation for language, philosophy, and critical thinking. The family home reverberated with lively debates, discussions, and the exploration of ideas, creating an intellectually stimulating environment that would shape Chomsky's formative years.

Education and Academic Influences

Noam Chomsky's educational journey began in earnest at the prestigious Oak Lane Country Day School, where he thrived academically and displayed an exceptional talent for learning languages. His voracious appetite for knowledge led him to delve into a myriad of subjects, ranging from mathematics to philosophy, nurturing an insatiable curiosity that would define his intellectual pursuits.

During his adolescence, Chomsky encountered the works of prominent philosophers such as Bertrand Russell and Rudolf Carnap, which further ignited his passion for understanding the nature of language and the mind. His encounters with the writings of linguists such as Zellig Harris and Roman Jakobson profoundly shaped his burgeoning fascination with the intricate mechanics of language.

Chomsky's thirst for academic enrichment led him to the hallowed halls of the University of Pennsylvania, where he embarked on a path of intellectual exploration. Under the tutelage of the eminent Zellig Harris, Chomsky immersed himself in the structuralist approach to linguistics, embracing its methodology and challenging its fundamental tenets. Guided by the legendary philosopher and cognitive scientist, Nelson Goodman, Chomsky began to cultivate his groundbreaking theory of transformational-generative grammar—a theory that would revolutionize the field of linguistics and establish him as a seminal figure in the realm of intellectual discourse.

At Harvard, where he conducted research for his doctoral thesis, Chomsky engaged with a vibrant community of scholars, including luminaries such as B.F. Skinner and W.V. Quine, whose ideas and debates shaped his understanding of psychology, philosophy, and the nature of human cognition. These encounters served as catalysts for Chomsky's multidisciplinary approach, inspiring him to transcend traditional academic boundaries and forge new paths of inquiry.

Chomsky's Linguistic Theories and Contributions

THE CHOMSKY HIERARCHY

Noam Chomsky embarked on a groundbreaking journey that would revolutionize the field of linguistics. He challenged the prevailing structuralist paradigm and set forth on a quest to develop a comprehensive framework that would illuminate the complexities of human communication.

Chomsky's seminal work led to the creation of the Chomsky Hierarchy, a groundbreaking classification system that categorizes formal languages into distinct levels of complexity. By hierarchically organizing languages based on their generative power, Chomsky introduced a framework that laid the foundation for understanding the limits and possibilities of human expression.

TRANSFORMATIONAL-GENERATIVE GRAMMAR

Central to Chomsky's linguistic theories is the concept of transformational-generative grammar, which seeks to uncover the underlying rules and structures that govern human language. Rejecting the behaviorist approach that dominated linguistic studies at the time, Chomsky advocated for a mentalistic framework that emphasized innate linguistic structures and the creative aspects of language use.

Chomsky's revolutionary theory posited that all human languages share a universal underlying structure, known as Universal Grammar. This innately endowed system of rules and principles enables individuals to acquire and generate infinite linguistic expressions, transcending the limitations of specific languages.

UNIVERSAL GRAMMAR

Chomsky's concept of Universal Grammar represented a monumental shift in linguistic thought. It suggested that despite the apparent diversity of languages across cultures, there exists a common underlying blueprint, a set of innate principles that guide language acquisition and production. Universal Grammar, as Chomsky argued, allows children to acquire language rapidly and effortlessly, navigating the intricacies of syntax, grammar, and semantics.

This revolutionary concept challenged the prevailing notion that language was solely a cultural construct. Chomsky's theories asserted that language is an inherent part of the human cognitive architecture, offering a window into the workings of the human mind and its innate capacity for linguistic creativity.

LANGUAGE ACQUISITION AND DEVELOPMENT

Chomsky's linguistic theories extended beyond the study of syntax and grammar. He delved into the complex processes of language acquisition and development, seeking to elucidate how children acquire language skills so effortlessly and rapidly.

Through meticulous research and analysis, Chomsky posited that language acquisition occurs through a combination of innate linguistic structures and exposure to linguistic input. Children possess an inherent capacity to analyze and internalize the linguistic patterns and structures of the language spoken around them, effortlessly constructing grammatically correct sentences without explicit instruction.

Chomsky's groundbreaking theories provided a new lens through which to understand the intricacies of language acquisition and development. They challenged conventional wisdom and sparked a paradigm shift, revolutionizing not only linguistics but also psychology, cognitive science, and education.

Chomsky's Political Activism and Thought

ANTI-WAR AND ANTI-IMPERIALISM

Chomsky, renowned for his linguistic prowess, demonstrated an unwavering commitment to using his intellectual platform to challenge prevailing power structures and advocate for social justice.

During the Vietnam War, Chomsky emerged as a fierce critic of U.S. military intervention. His opposition to the war was grounded in a deep sense of moral conviction and an astute analysis of U.S. foreign policy. Through incisive speeches, essays, and public engagements, Chomsky exposed the true nature of American imperialism, highlighting the devastating human consequences and the erosion of civil liberties in the pursuit of global dominance.

ANARCHISM AND LIBERTARIAN SOCIALISM

Chomsky's political ideology was rooted in his firm belief in the principles of anarchism and libertarian socialism. Drawing inspiration from political philosophers such as Mikhail Bakunin and Peter Kropotkin, Chomsky championed a vision of society free from hierarchical systems of power and domination.

His advocacy for anarchism was not a call for chaos, but rather a quest for a just society based on voluntary cooperation and shared decision-making. Chomsky envisioned a world where individuals had agency over their lives and collective action was guided by principles of equity and solidarity.

CRITICISM OF U.S. FOREIGN POLICY

Chomsky's penetrating analysis of U.S. foreign policy laid bare the often-hidden realities of American global engagement.

He condemned the United States' support for repressive regimes, its covert operations, and its military interventions that perpetuated suffering and undermined democracy in various regions around the world. Chomsky's scathing critique of U.S. foreign policy extended beyond mere criticism; it was a call to hold those in power accountable for their actions. He questioned the motivations behind American interventions, exposing the interests of corporate power, resource exploitation, and geopolitical dominance that lay beneath the veneer of humanitarian rhetoric.

INFLUENCE ON ACTIVIST AND RADICAL MOVEMENTS

Chomsky's intellectual and political contributions transcended academia, resonating deeply with activists and radical movements worldwide. His analyses, impassioned speeches, and writings became rallying cries for those seeking social justice and systemic change.

His relentless pursuit of truth and his unwavering commitment to challenging established power structures inspired countless individuals to question the status quo. Chomsky's work on media analysis, in particular, shed light on the propagandistic nature of mainstream media, empowering citizens to critically engage with information and seek alternative narratives.

Through his lectures, interviews, and participation in grassroots movements, Chomsky became a mentor and guiding light for generations of activists, fostering a legacy of intellectual dissent and resistance to injustice.

Chomsky's Other Academic Contributions

COGNITIVE SCIENCE AND PSYCHOLOGY

Drawing upon his deep understanding of language, Chomsky ventured into the territory of the human mind, seeking to unravel its intricate workings. His exploration of cognitive science shed light on how humans acquire, process, and generate knowledge. Chomsky's theories on language acquisition, in particular, challenged prevailing behaviorist models and emphasized the role of innate cognitive structures. His research and writings provided a framework for understanding the mental processes underlying language production, perception, and comprehension.

PHILOSOPHY AND ETHICS

It was only natural that Chomsky's curiosity led him to philosophy and ethics, where he grappled with fundamental questions about human existence and morality.

Deeply influenced by thinkers such as Immanuel Kant and John Dewey, Chomsky pondered the foundations of ethical systems and explored the intersection between language, thought, and moral reasoning.

His work on universal grammar and the innateness of language highlighted the universality of certain moral principles, challenging relativistic notions and suggesting a shared ethical foundation among humans. Chomsky's philosophical insights provided a powerful lens through which to examine the ethical dimensions of societal structures, politics, and power dynamics.

COMPUTATIONAL SCIENCE AND ARTIFICIAL INTELLIGENCE

Chomsky's scholarly pursuits extended into the realm of exploring the capacity of machines to simulate human intelligence and language. Within this domain, his contributions intersected with his linguistic theories, providing valuable insights into the intricacies of language processing and the inherent limitations of computer-based systems.

Questioning the notion of strong artificial intelligence, which suggests that machines can possess true human-like intelligence, Chomsky's skepticism challenged prevailing beliefs.

He argued that although computers can excel at specific tasks, the essence of human cognition and the richness of human language remain elusive to replication.

Through his exploration of computational science and artificial intelligence, Chomsky shed light on the frontiers of human cognition, igniting profound discussions and debates about the nature of intelligence and the potential limits of technological advancement.

Noam Chomsky's multidisciplinary forays into cognitive science, psychology, philosophy, and computational science showcased his intellectual versatility and insatiable thirst for knowledge. Chomsky's intellectual breadth solidifies his legacy as a true polymath and a formidable force in shaping our understanding of the human experience.

Personal Life

Behind his brilliant mind and big ideas, Noam Chomsky's personal life shows a kind heart and the relationships that shaped him. Chomsky's marriage to his wife, Carol, served as a steadfast anchor in his life. They married in 1949, remained together until her passing in 2008, and had three children together. In 2014, he married Valeria Wasserman, a translator and political activist from Brazil.

Despite being a public figure known for his intellectual and political contributions, Noam Chomsky has maintained a strong preference for privacy in his personal life, keeping his personal relationships out of the public spotlight while focusing primarily on his work and activism.

Influence and Legacy

Noam Chomsky's impact transcends the realms of linguistics and politics, leaving an indelible imprint on both fields. His linguistic theories revolutionized the study of language, reshaping the foundations of linguistic thought and challenging established paradigms.

In the political arena, Chomsky's unyielding commitment to social justice, his fervent critique of power structures, and his unwavering advocacy for peace and equality resonated deeply with activists and scholars alike. His writings and speeches became essential texts for those seeking to understand the complexities of global politics, U.S. foreign policy, and the intersection of power and ideology.

Chomsky's legacy as an intellectual giant continues to reverberate through academia, activism, and beyond. The breadth of his ideas and the depth of his intellectual engagement ensure a lasting influence that will continue to shape the intellectual landscape for generations to come.

The general
population doesn't
know what's happening,
and it doesn't even
know that it doesn't
know.

Noam Chomsky's
little book of
selected quotes

I try to encourage people to think for themselves, to question standard assumptions... Don't take assumptions for granted. Begin by taking a skeptical attitude toward anything that is conventional wisdom. Make it justify itself. It usually can't. Be willing to ask questions about what is taken for granted. Try to think things through for yourself.

Democratic societies can't force people. Therefore they have to control what they think.

Capitalism denies the right to live. You have only the right to remain on the labour market.

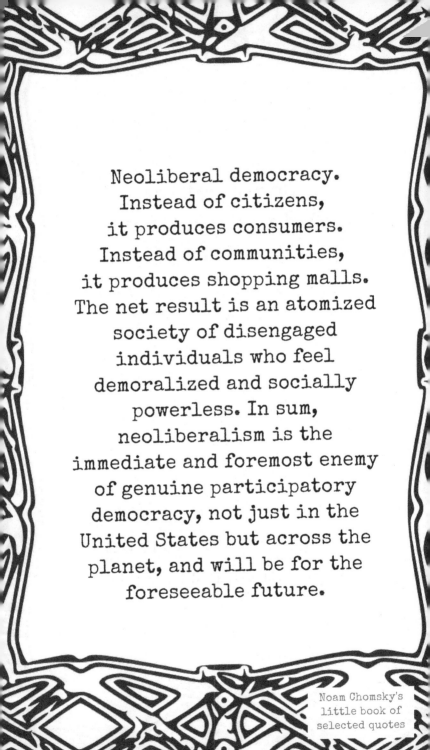

Neoliberal democracy.
Instead of citizens,
it produces consumers.
Instead of communities,
it produces shopping malls.
The net result is an atomized
society of disengaged
individuals who feel
demoralized and socially
powerless. In sum,
neoliberalism is the
immediate and foremost enemy
of genuine participatory
democracy, not just in the
United States but across the
planet, and will be for the
foreseeable future.

Technology is basically neutral. It's kind of like a hammer. The hammer doesn't care whether you use it to build a house, or whether a torturer uses it to crush somebody's skull.

Noam Chomsky's little book of selected quotes

There's a good
reason why nobody
studies history,
it just teaches you
too much.

Education is a
system of imposed
ignorance.

Noam Chomsky's
little book of
selected quotes

The smart way to keep people passive and obedient is to strictly limit the spectrum of acceptable opinion, but allow very lively debate within that spectrum – even encourage the more critical and dissident views. That gives people the sense that there's free thinking going on, while all the time the presuppositions of the system are being reinforced by the limits put on the range of the debate.

Noam Chomsky's little book of selected quotes

In a capitalist system, there's a principle that if you invest, especially in a long-term risky investment, if something comes out of it, you're supposed to get the profit. It doesn't happen in our system. The taxpayer paid for it and gets nothing – assumes all of the risk, gets zero. The money goes into the pockets of Bill Gates and Steve Jobs, who are ripping off decades of work in the public sector.

Noam Chomsky's little book of selected quotes

How it is we have so much information, but know so little?

Efforts can succeed over time, and not trying ensures that the worst will happen.

Noam Chomsky's little book of selected quotes

Students who acquire large debts putting themselves through school are unlikely to think about changing society. When you trap people in a system of debt, they can't afford the time to think. Tuition fee increases are a disciplinary technique, and by the time students graduate, they are not only loaded with debt, but have also internalized the disciplinarian culture. This makes them efficient components of the consumer economy.

Noam Chomsky's little book of selected quotes

It's ridiculous to talk about freedom in a society dominated by huge corporations. What kind of freedom is there inside a corporation? They're totalitarian institutions – you take orders from above and maybe give them to people below you. There's about as much freedom as under Stalinism.

The media want to maintain their intimate relation to state power. They want to get leaks, they want to get invited to the press conferences. They want to rub shoulders with the Secretary of State, all that kind of business. To do that, you've got to play the game, and playing the game means telling their lies, serving as their disinformation apparatus.

Noam Chomsky's little book of selected quotes

We shouldn't be
looking for heroes,
we should be looking
for good ideas.

One of the greatest
dangers is secular
religion – state
worship.

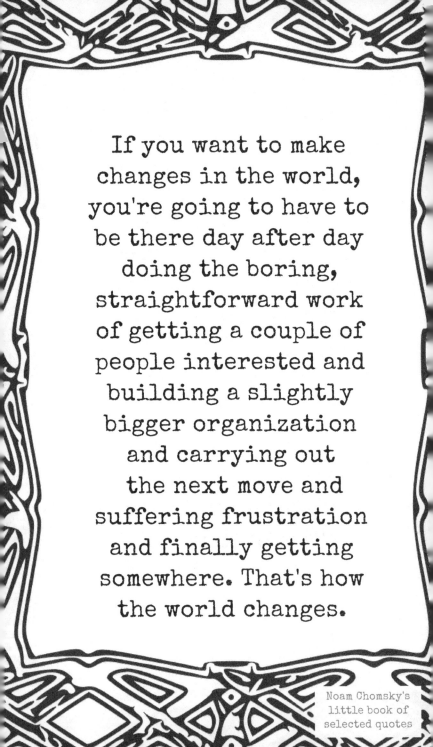

If you want to make changes in the world, you're going to have to be there day after day doing the boring, straightforward work of getting a couple of people interested and building a slightly bigger organization and carrying out the next move and suffering frustration and finally getting somewhere. That's how the world changes.

Noam Chomsky's little book of selected quotes

For the powerful, crimes are those that others commit.

People are capable of seeing the deceit they're ensnared in. They just have to make the effort.

Goebbels was in favor of free speech for views he liked. So was Stalin. If you're really in favor of free speech, then you're in favor of freedom of speech for precisely the views you despise. Otherwise, you're not in favor of free speech.

Noam Chomsky's little book of selected quotes

When I was in high school I asked myself at one point: "Why do I care if my high school's team wins the football game? I don't know anybody on the team, they have nothing to do with me... why am I here and applaud? It does not make any sense." But the point is, it does make sense: It's a way of building up irrational attitudes of submission to authority and group cohesion behind leadership elements. In fact it's training in irrational jingoism. That's also a feature of competitive sports.

Noam Chomsky's little book of selected quotes

In the US, there is basically one party – the business party. It has two factions, called Democrats and Republicans, which are somewhat different but carry out variations on the same policies. By and large, I am opposed to those policies. As is most of the population.

A language is not just words. It's a culture, a tradition, a unification of a community, a whole history that creates what a community is. It's all embodied in a language.

If you want to control a population... give them a God to worship.

It is the responsibility of intellectuals to speak the truth and expose lies.

Noam Chomsky's little book of selected quotes

The search for truth is a cooperative, unending endeavor. We can, and should, engage in it to the extent we can and encourage others to do so as well, seeking to free ourselves from constraints imposed by coercive institutions, dogma, irrationality, excessive conformity and lack of initiative and imagination, and numerous other obstacles.

Citizens of
the democratic
societies should
undertake a course
of intellectual self
defense to protect
themselves from
manipulation and
control, and to lay
the basis for
meaningful
democracy.

Noam Chomsky's
little book of
selected quotes

The point of public relations slogans like "Support Our Troops" is that they don't mean anything ... that's the whole point of good propaganda. You want to create a slogan that nobody is going to be against and I suppose everybody will be for, because nobody knows what it means, because it doesn't mean anything. But its crucial value is that it diverts your attention from a question that does mean something, do you support our policy? And that's the one you're not allowed to talk about.

The best defense
against democracy is
to distract people.

You cannot control
your own population
by force, but it can
be distracted by
consumption. The
business press has
been quite explicit
about this goal.

That's the standard technique of privatization: defund, make sure things don't work, people get angry, you hand it over to private capital.

Noam Chomsky's little book of selected quotes

Nobody is going to pour truth into your brain. It's something you have to find out for yourself.

See, people with power understand exactly one thing: violence.

Noam Chomsky's little book of selected quotes

If the Nuremberg laws were applied, then every post-war American president would have been hanged.

Noam Chomsky's little book of selected quotes

The goal is to keep
the bewildered herd
bewildered.
It's unnecessary
for them to trouble
themselves with what's
happening in the world.
In fact, it's undesirable
– if they see too much of
reality they may set
themselves to change it.

Noam Chomsky's
little book of
selected quotes

It's pretty ironic that the so-called 'least advanced' people are the ones taking the lead in trying to protect all of us, while the richest and most powerful among us are the ones who are trying to drive the society to destruction.

Noam Chomsky's little book of selected quotes

The police can go to downtown Harlem and pick up a kid with a joint in the streets. But they can't go into the elegant apartments and get a stockbroker who's sniffing cocaine.

The whole educational and professional training system is a very elaborate filter, which just weeds out people who are too independent, and who think for themselves, and who don't know how to be submissive, and so on -- because they're dysfunctional to the institutions.

Noam Chomsky's little book of selected quotes

The public is not to see where power lies, how it shapes policy, and for what ends. Rather, people are to hate and fear one another.

Noam Chomsky's little book of selected quotes

Jingoism, racism, fear, religious fundamentalism: these are the ways of appealing to people if you're trying to organize a mass base of support for policies that are really intended to crush them.

Noam Chomsky's little book of selected quotes

If you are not offending people who ought to be offended, you're doing something wrong.

To live a life of honesty and integrity is a responsibility of every decent person.

Noam Chomsky's little book of selected quotes

If you go to one demonstration and then go home, that's something, but the people in power can live with that. What they can't live with is sustained pressure that keeps building, organisations that keep doing things, people that keep learning lessons from the last time and doing it better the next time.

Noam Chomsky's little book of selected quotes

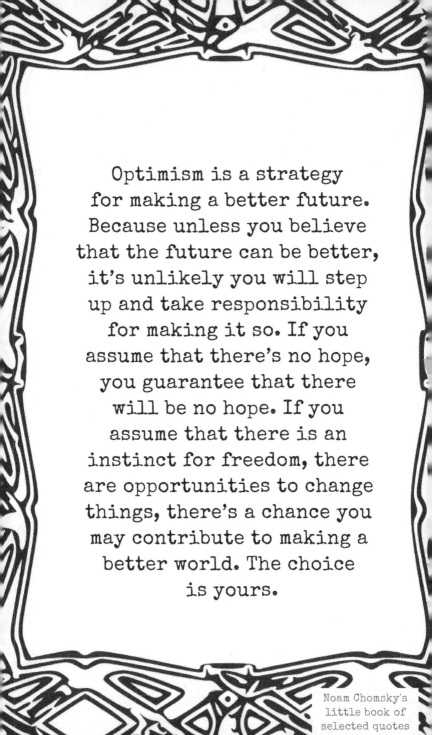

Optimism is a strategy
for making a better future.
Because unless you believe
that the future can be better,
it's unlikely you will step
up and take responsibility
for making it so. If you
assume that there's no hope,
you guarantee that there
will be no hope. If you
assume that there is an
instinct for freedom, there
are opportunities to change
things, there's a chance you
may contribute to making a
better world. The choice
is yours.

Noam Chomsky's
little book of
selected quotes

The threat of China is not military. The threat of China is they can't be intimidated. Europe you can intimidate. When the US tries to get people to stop investing in Iran, European companies pull out, China disregards it. You look at history and understand why – they've been around for 4,000 years, they have contempt for the barbarians, they just don't give a damn.

Noam Chomsky's little book of selected quotes

If we don't believe
in free expression
for people we
despise, we don't
believe in it at all.

If something is
repeated over and
over as obvious, the
chances are that it
is obviously false.

Noam Chomsky's
little book of
selected quotes

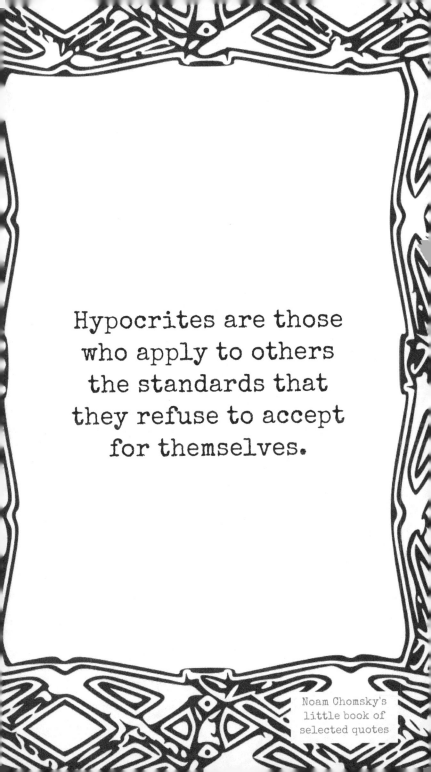

Hypocrites are those who apply to others the standards that they refuse to accept for themselves.

As long as the general population is passive, apathetic, diverted to consumerism or hatred of the vulnerable, then the powerful can do as they please, and those who survive will be left to contemplate the outcome.

The key element of social control is the strategy of distraction that is to divert public attention from important issues and changes decided by political and economic elites, through the technique of flood or flooding continuous distractions and insignificant information.

Noam Chomsky's little book of selected quotes

I don't bother writing about Fox News. It is too easy. What I talk about are the liberal intellectuals, the ones who portray themselves and perceive themselves as challenging power, as courageous, as standing up for truth and justice. They are basically the guardians of the faith. They set the limits. They tell us how far we can go. They say, 'Look how courageous I am.' But do not go one millimeter beyond that. At least for the educated sectors, they are the most dangerous in supporting power.

Noam Chomsky's little book of selected quotes

Some journalists will tell you, and they're correct, that nobody is ordering them to do anything. That's right. Nobody is ordering them to do anything. The indoctrination is so deep that educated people think they're being objective.

The world is a very puzzling place. If you're not willing to be puzzled, you just become a replica of someone else's mind.

Noam Chomsky's little book of selected quotes

Anyone who studies declassified documents soon becomes aware that government secrecy is largely an effort to protect policy makers from scrutiny by citizens, not to protect the country from enemies.

Noam Chomsky's little book of selected quotes

For those who stubbornly seek freedom, there can be no more urgent task than to come to understand the mechanisms and practices of indoctrination.

States are not
moral agents,
people are,
and can impose
moral standards
on powerful
institutions.

When Israelis in the occupied territories now claim that they have to defend themselves, they are defending themselves in the sense that any military occupier has to defend itself against the population they are crushing. You can't defend yourself when you're militarily occupying someone else's land. That's not defense. Call it what you like, it's not defense.

It takes one minute
to tell a lie, and an
hour to refute it.

Do you train for
passing tests or
do you train for
creative inquiry?

Noam Chomsky's
little book of
selected quotes

We still name our military helicopter gunships after victims of genocide. Nobody bats an eyelash about that: Blackhawk. Apache. And Comanche. If the Luftwaffe named its military helicopters Jew and Gypsy, I suppose people would notice.

Noam Chomsky's little book of selected quotes

The business classes are very class-conscious—they're constantly fighting a bitter class war to improve their power and diminish opposition. Occasionally this is recognized. We don't use the term "working class" here [in the U.S] because it's a taboo term. You're supposed to say "middle class," because it helps diminish the understanding that there's a class war going on.

Noam Chomsky's little book of selected quotes

The United States happens to be the only state in the world that has been condemned by the World Court for international terrorism.

Noam Chomsky's little book of selected quotes

I mean, it's true, nobody talks about them, but when you bring it up, the idea that you have to rent yourself to somebody and follow their orders, and that they own and you work there, and you built it but you don't own it, that's a highly unnatural notion. You don't have to study any complicated theories to see that this is an attack on human dignity.

Noam Chomsky's little book of selected quotes

Capitalism is a system in which the central institutions of society are, in principle, under autocratic control. Thus, a corporation or an industry is, if we were to think of it in political terms, fascist, that is, it has tight control at the top and strict obedience has to be established at every level. [...] Just as I'm opposed to political fascism, I am opposed to economic fascism. I think that until the major institutions of society are under the popular control of participants and communities, it's pointless to talk about democracy.

The more you can increase fear of drugs and crime, welfare mothers, immigrants and aliens, the more you control all the people.

Noam Chomsky's little book of selected quotes

It is a virtual reflex
for governments to
plead security concerns
when they undertake any
controversial action,
often as a pretext for
something else.

Noam Chomsky's
little book of
selected quotes

If anybody thinks they should listen to me because I'm a professor at MIT, that's nonsense. You should decide whether something makes sense by its content, not by the letters after the name of the person who says it.

Noam Chomsky's little book of selected quotes

All public
resources go to the
rich. The poor, if
they can survive in
the labor market,
fine. Otherwise,
they die. That's
economics in a
nutshell.

The leading student of business propaganda, Australian social scientist Alex Carey, argues persuasively that "the 20th century has been characterized by three developments of great political importance: the growth of democracy, the growth of corporate power, and the growth of corporate propaganda as a means of protecting corporate power against democracy."

It doesn't matter
how much you
learn in school;
it's whether you
learn how to go on
and do things by
yourself. And that
can be done at
any level.

Noam Chomsky's
little book of
selected quotes

Karl Marx said, "The task is not just to understand the world but to change it." A variant to keep in mind is that if you want to change the world you'd better try to understand it. That doesn't mean listening to a talk or reading a book, though that's helpful sometimes. You learn from participating. You learn from others. You learn from the people you're trying to organize. We all have to gain the understanding and the experience to formulate and implement ideas.

If there are dollars to be made,
you destroy the environment. The
reason is elementary. The people
who are going to be harmed by this
are your grandchildren and they
don't have any votes in the market.
Their interests are worth zero.
Anybody that pays attention to
their grandchildren's interests
is being irrational. Because what
you're supposed to do is maximize
your own interests, measured by
wealth, right now. Nothing else
matters. So destroying the
environment and militarizing
outer space are rational policies,
but within a framework of
institutional lunacy.

Noam Chomsky's
little book of
selected quotes

It's very common
for the victims to
understand a system
better than the
people who are
holding the stick.

Noam Chomsky's
little book of
selected quotes

Every great power,
every aggressive
power has always
regarded itself as
exceptional and as
doing things only for
the most moral ends.

Noam Chomsky's
little book of
selected quotes

You keep plugging away--that's the way social change takes place. That's the way every social change in history has taken place: by a lot of people, who nobody ever heard of, doing work.

Moral cowardice
and intellectual
corruption are the
natural concomitants
of unchallenged
privilege.

Noam Chomsky's
little book of
selected quotes

There are very few
people who are going
to look into the
mirror and say,
'That person I see
is a savage monster;'
instead, they make up
some construction that
justifies what they do.

Noam Chomsky's
little book of
selected quotes

In our society, real power does not happen to lie in the political system, it lies in the private economy: that's where the decisions are made about what's produced, how much is produced, what's consumed, where investment takes place, who has jobs, who controls the resources, and so on and so forth. And as long as that remains the case, changes inside the political system can make some difference—I don't want to say it's zero—but the differences are going to be very slight.

The general public
are not even aware
of major decisions
that will determine
their fate, hence
are in no position
to influence them.

What is called 'capitalism' is basically a system of corporate mercantilism, with huge and largely unaccountable private tyrannies exercising vast control over the economy, political systems, and social and cultural life, operating in close cooperation with powerful states that intervene massively in the domestic economy and international society.

Noam Chomsky's little book of selected quotes

The most effective way to restrict democracy is to transfer decision-making from the public arena to unaccountable institutions: kings and princes, priestly castes, military juntas, party dictatorships, or modern corporations.

Noam Chomsky's little book of selected quotes

One might ask why
tobacco is legal
and marijuana not.
A possible answer is
suggested by the nature
of the crop. Marijuana
can be grown almost
anywhere, with little
difficulty. It might not
be easily marketable by
major corporations.
Tobacco is quite
another story.

Noam Chomsky's
little book of
selected quotes

A basic principle
of modern state
capitalism is that
costs and risks are
socialized to the
extent possible,
while profit is
privatized.

Noam Chomsky's
little book of
selected quotes

If by 'intellectual' you mean people who are a special class who are in the business of imposing thoughts and forming ideas for people in power, and telling people what they should believe...they're really more a kind of secular priesthood, whose task it is to uphold the doctrinal truths of the society. And the population should be anti-intellectual in that respect.

There's no more
morality in
world affairs,
fundamentally,
than there was
at the time of
Genghis Khan.

Noam Chomsky's
little book of
selected quotes

"Growth" is a funny sort of concept. For example, our GNP increases every time we build a prison. Well, okay, it's growth in a sense, but it's kind of a dumb measure. Has our life improved if we have more people in prison?

Noam Chomsky's little book of selected quotes

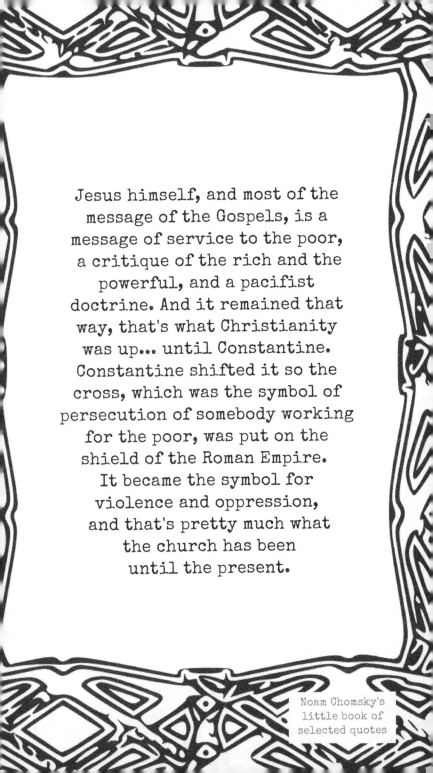

Jesus himself, and most of the message of the Gospels, is a message of service to the poor, a critique of the rich and the powerful, and a pacifist doctrine. And it remained that way, that's what Christianity was up... until Constantine. Constantine shifted it so the cross, which was the symbol of persecution of somebody working for the poor, was put on the shield of the Roman Empire. It became the symbol for violence and oppression, and that's pretty much what the church has been until the present.

Noam Chomsky's little book of selected quotes

Power is concentrated.
The general policy is
exactly the way that
Adam Smith described it:
it's designed for the
benefit of its principal
architects, the powerful.
It serves "the vile maxim
of the masters: all for
ourselves and nothing
for anyone else". Those
are the basic rules
of the world.

Noam Chomsky's
little book of
selected quotes

Control of thought is more important for governments that are free and popular than for despotic and military states. The logic is straightforward: a despotic state can control its domestic enemies by force, but as the state loses this weapon, other devices are required to prevent the ignorant masses from interfering with public affairs, which are none of their business... the public are to be observers, not participants, consumers of ideology as well as products.

Noam Chomsky's little book of selected quotes

There is a social responsibility to take care of vulnerable people. It seems that a sensible social responsibility is obligatory education, but also decent education, and that is not happening.

Noam Chomsky's little book of selected quotes

If there was an observer on Mars, they would probably be amazed that we have survived this long. There are two problems for our species' survival – nuclear war and environmental catastrophe – and we're hurtling towards them. Knowingly. This hypothetical Martian would probably conclude that human beings were an evolutionary error.

Noam Chomsky's little book of selected quotes

Concentration
of wealth yields
concentration
of political power.
And concentration of
political power gives
rise to legislation
that increases and
accelerates the cycle.

Noam Chomsky's
little book of
selected quotes

Far from creating independent thinkers, schools have always, throughout history, played an institutional role in a system of control and coercion. And once you are well educated you have already been socialized in ways that support the power structure, which, in turn, rewards you immensely.

Noam Chomsky's little book of selected quotes

I have no Facebook page or Twitter – I don't participate in it, and I don't like it particularly. I mean, it's a form of interaction, which strikes me as extremely superficial.

Noam Chomsky's little book of selected quotes

Africa's a wreck and it's not because it was hit by an asteroid. It's a wreck largely because it was hit by Europe.

Noam Chomsky's little book of selected quotes

If you care about other people, you might try to organize to undermine power and authority. That's not going to happen if you care only about yourself.

In the early 1940s, as a young teenager, I was utterly appalled by the racist and jingoist hysteria of the anti-Japanese propaganda. The Germans were evil, but treated with some respect: They were, after all, blond Aryan types, just like our imaginary self-image. Japanese were mere vermin, to be crushed like ants.

Globalization is the result of powerful governments, especially that of the United States, pushing trade deals and other accords down the throats of the world's people to make it easier for corporations and the wealthy to dominate the economies of nations around the world without having obligations to the peoples of those nations.

Noam Chomsky's little book of selected quotes

A captured pirate was brought before the emperor Alexander the Great; "How dare you molest the sea?" asked Alexander. "How dare you molest the whole world" replied the pirate, who continued, "Because I do it with a little ship only, I am called a thief; you, doing it with a great navy, are called an emperor."

Noam Chomsky's little book of selected quotes

If you are working 50 hours a week in a factory, you don't have time to read 10 newspapers a day and go back to declassified government archives. But such people may have far-reaching insights into the way the world works.

Noam Chomsky's little book of selected quotes

The notion 'grammatical' cannot be identified with 'meaningful' or 'significant' in any semantic sense. Sentences (1) and (2) are equally nonsensical, but...only the former is grammatical.
(1) Colourless green ideas sleep furiously.
(2) Furiously sleep ideas green colourless.

Noam Chomsky's little book of selected quotes

The costs of the Bush-Obama wars in Iraq and Afghanistan are now estimated to run as high as $4.4 trillion – a major victory for Osama bin Laden, whose announced goal was to bankrupt America by drawing it into a trap. The 2011 military budget – almost matching that of the rest of the world combined – is higher in real terms than at any time since World War II and is slated to go even higher.

Hume's paradox does hold: power is in the hands of the governed. If they refuse to accept it, you're in trouble, no matter how many guns you have.

Noam Chomsky's little book of selected quotes

The first step is to penetrate the clouds of deceit and distortion and learn the truth about the world, then to organize and act to change it. That's never been impossible and never been easy.

Noam Chomsky's little book of selected quotes

A consistent anarchist must oppose private ownership of the means of production, and the wage-slavery which is a component of this system, as incompatible with the principle that labor must be freely undertaken and under the control of the producer.

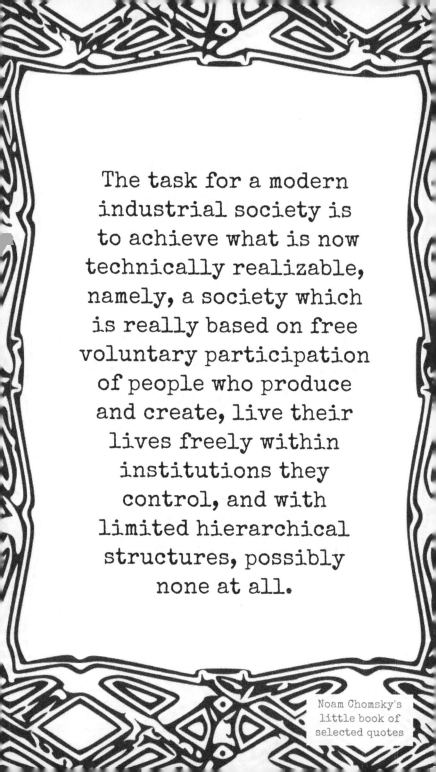

The task for a modern industrial society is to achieve what is now technically realizable, namely, a society which is really based on free voluntary participation of people who produce and create, live their lives freely within institutions they control, and with limited hierarchical structures, possibly none at all.

Noam Chomsky's little book of selected quotes